AMERICA GOES TO WAR

WORLD WAR II
IN EUROPE AND NORTH AFRICA
TIMELINES, FACTS, AND BATTLES

By Craig Boutland

Published in 2023 by The Rosen Publishing Group, Inc.
2544 Clinton Street, Buffalo, NY 14224

Editor: Lindsey Lowe
Children's Publisher: Anne O'Daly
Design Manager: Keith Davis
Picture Manager: Sophie Mortimer

Picture Credits:
Front Cover:Everett Collection/Shutterstock.com
Key: t = top, b = bottom, c = center
Alamy: 502 Collection 26, United Archives GmbH 13, 15, World of Triss 25b; Nick Cornish: 29, 47b; German Federal Archives: Bundersarchiv bild 16-17, 17t, 22b, 33t; Getty Images: 11t; Imperial War Museum: 20, 22t, 38, 39t, 38-39, 39; Lebrecht Collection: 12, 14, 15b, 40, 46; National Portrait Gallery: 23t; Public Domain: 10t, 10b, 11b, 23b, 32b, 48t, 54, Auschwitzerkennungsdienst 48-49, Batume Gendame Administration 32t, Center for Jewish history NYC 49c; Robert Hunt Library: 5, 6,7,8, 9,15t, 16b, 17b, 18, 19t, 21, 25t, 27t, 28, 34, 35, 36, 37, 39cl, 41, 42, 44, 45b, 47t, 50, 51, 52, 53; Topfoto: 19b, 24, 27b, 30, 45t; United States Government: National Archives 33b, U.S. Army Center of Military History 17cl, U.S. Army Photograph 49t.

Cataloging-in-Publication Data

Names: Boutland, Craig.
Title: World War II in Europe and North Africa: timelines, facts, and battles / Craig Boutland.
Description: New York : Rosen Publishing, 2023. | Series: America goes to war| Includes bibliographic references, index and glossary.
Identifiers: ISBN 9781499473971 (pbk) | ISBN 9781499473988 (library bound) | ISBN 9781499473995 (ebook)
Subjects: LCSH: World War, 1935-1945—Europe —Juvenile literature | World War, 1935-1945—North Africa —Juvenile literature
Classification: LCC D756 B68 2023 | DDC 940.54—dc23

Manufactured in the United States of America

CPSIA Compliance Information: Batch #CWRYA23. For further information contact Rosen Publishing at 1-800-237-9932.

CONTENTS

Introduction

World War II was the largest and most destructive war in history. Between 1939 and 1945, 100 million troops were mobilized across the world.

As many as 60 million people died in the conflict. Most were civilians who died as a result of bombing, starvation, disease, or persecution by brutal regimes. The biggest crime against civilians was the murder of six million Jews by the Nazis.

The Course of the War

Adolf Hitler's Nazi Party came to power in Germany in 1933 promising territorial expansion. Hitler's invasion of Poland on September 1, 1939, brought declarations of war from France and from Britain and its empire. Using a tactic known as blitzkrieg (lightning war), the Germans soon conquered much of Europe, dragging most of the continent into the war.

In June 1941 Hitler invaded the Soviet Union. Later that year, the United States entered the war after Germany's ally, Japan, bombed the U.S. Pacific base at Pearl Harbor. The Allies agreed to prioritize the war in Europe and planned a landing in northern France that eventually took place in June 1944. Meanwhile, British and U.S. troops had defeated the Axis in North Africa and advanced up the Italian peninsula; the Soviet Red Army had turned back the Germans and was heading west. The two fronts closed on Berlin, where Hitler shot himself amid the ruins of his empire shortly before Germany surrendered.

About This Book

This book focuses on the war in Europe and North Africa from 1939 to 1945. It contains two types of timelines. Along the bottom of the pages is a timeline that covers the whole period. It lists key events and developments, including from the Pacific War, color coded. Each chapter also has its own timeline, which runs vertically down the sides of the pages. This timeline provides more specific information about the particular subject of the chapter. IN FOCUS spreads give more details of personalities, weapons, and key events.

A convoy of Allied merchant ships crosses the Atlantic Ocean. Ships traveled together so they were easier to protect from attack by German U-boats.

Why the War Began

Hitler was determined to bring together the lands of German-speaking people. His campaign of territorial expansion took Europe into war.

German troops remove a barrier at a border crossing as they invade Poland on September 1, 1939.

TIMELINE 1939 JANUARY–JUNE

KEY: Politics | Land War | Sea and Air War

January

January 26 Spain Nationalists capture Barcelona, the Republican-held capital of Catalonia.

February

March

March 10 Czechoslovakia Hitler begins the takeover of Bohemia and Moravia, home to many Germans. The operation is over by March 16; Czechoslovakia no longer exists.

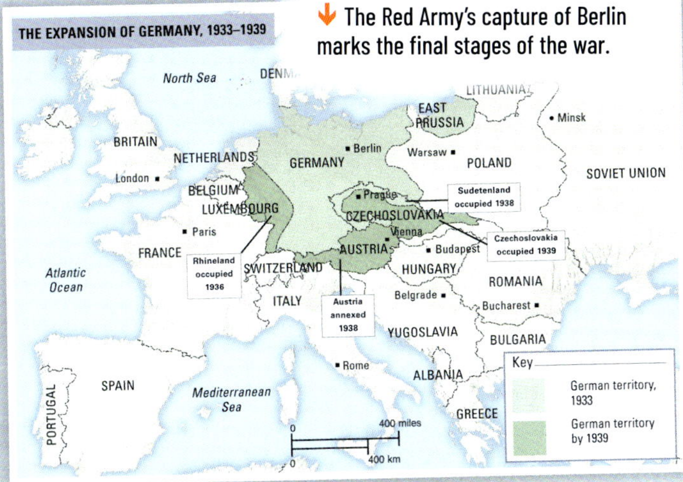

The Red Army's capture of Berlin marks the final stages of the war.

Adolf Hitler came to power in Germany in 1933 saying he would reject what Germans saw as the unfair peace treaties that ended World War I in 1918. Hitler was determined to expand Germany to include the large German populations living in other countries. He rearmed Germany and occupied the Rhineland. Hitler's move was a gamble, but the neighboring French did nothing. They were waiting for support from Britain. The British, however, were suspicious of France's alliance with the Soviet Union.

KEY DATES

March 1938 Anschluss ("Union") between Germany and Austria.

September 1938 The Munich Conference agrees to Germany's occupation of the Sudetenland.

March 1939 Hitler occupies the rest of Czechoslovakia.

May 1939 Germany and Italy form the "Pact of Steel."

August 1939 Germany signs a nonaggression pact with the Soviet Union.

September 1, 1939 German forces invade Poland.

September 3, 1939 Britain, France, and their allies declare war on Germany.

Edvard Beneš, Czech president, opposed Nazi Germany's claim to the Sudetenland. Without support from other nations, he had to give in to Adolf Hitler's demands.

May 22 Italy The Italian government forges stronger ties with Germany in what is known as the "Pact of Steel."

April

May

June

March 28 Spain Nationalist troops enter Madrid, marking the end of a civil war in which 300,000 Spaniards have died; General Francisco Franco takes over the government.

Munich Conference

British Prime Minister Neville Chamberlain called a conference in Munich in 1938 to try to avoid war. He thought that if the Allies gave in to Hitler's demands for the return of "German" lands, Hitler would not go to war. But Hitler saw "appeasement" as a sign of weakness and proof that the Allies would not intervene if he took over Czechoslovakia.

German troops enter the Rhineland on March 7, 1936.

Rome-Berlin Axis

In October 1936, Italian dictator Benito Mussolini and Hitler formed the Rome–Berlin Axis. Italy's support allowed Hitler to declare Austria a province of the German Reich, or empire, in March 1938, the so-called "Anschluss" (Union).

The democracies' failure to act encouraged Hitler to target the Sudetenland, a Czech border area where many Germans lived. At an international conference at Munich in September 1938, Hitler got his way. The Czechs were told to leave the Sudetenland. Hitler now believed that neither Britain

Mussolini and Hitler, at left, face Chamberlain (far right) in Munich in September 1938.

TIMELINE 1939 JULY–DECEMBER

KEY: Politics | Land War | Sea and Air War

August 23 Germany The Nazi government signs a nonaggression pact with the Soviet Union. The Soviets will allow Germany to invade Poland; in return, Germany will divide Poland with the Soviet Union.

September 1 Poland
A large German force invades; with few tanks or aircraft, Poland is quickly overwhelmed.

July — August — September

September 3 Europe
Britain, France, Australia, and New Zealand declare war on Nazi Germany.

→ German troops march into the town square of Friedland on October 3, 1938.

nor France would fight. In March 1939, his troops occupied the rest of Czechoslovakia.

Poland

Now Hitler turned to Poland, which included two areas that were home to about a million Germans. To avoid a possible alliance between Britain, France, and the Soviet Union, Hitler made a pact with Stalin's Soviet Union (see right). The western democracies decided to make a stand, however. Britain and France offered to guarantee Polish independence.

On August 31, SS troops in Polish uniforms staged a mock raid on a radio station in the German border town of Gleiwitz. Hitler used the "raid" as an excuse to invade Poland on September 1, 1939. Two days later, France and Britain declared war on Germany, as did Britain's dependencies. World War II had begun.

Hitler and Stalin

The failure of France and Britain to halt Hitler's demands at Munich had an important effect on Soviet leader Josef Stalin. He decided he had to cope with German expansion eastward without their help.
In August 1939, Stalin signed a nonaggression pact with Germany, which included a deal to divide Poland between them in the event of war. The agreement between fascism on one side and communism on the other shocked the world. It also left Hitler with a free hand in Poland.

October — November — December

September 18–30 Poland Poland is defeated and split into German and Soviet zones of occupation; many Poles escape.

October 14 North Sea A U-boat (submarine) sinks the battleship HMS *Royal Oak* in the British base at Scapa Flow, with the loss of 786 lives.

November 30 Finland Some 600,000 Soviet troops invade Finland. Despite inferior numbers, the Finns hold the invaders at the Mannerheim Line. Soviet troops struggle because they have poor winter clothes.

December 13 Atlantic Ocean The British trap the German pocket battleship *Graf Spee* at the mouth of the River Plate, Uruguay; the damaged ship is scuttled (sunk) by its crew a few days later.

December 14 Finland The League of Nations expels the Soviet Union after it fails to halt the war in Finland.

Fascism and Strong Leaders in Europe

Over much of Europe, the lure of the strong leader proved irresistible during the 1920s and 1930s.

In the confusion that followed the end of World War I there were communist revolutions throughout Europe in imitation of the regime in Russia. Although none of them succeeded, they added to a sense of the fragile nature of the many new states that were created from the former empires of Russia, Germany, Austria-Hungary, and Turkey, which had collapsed at the war's end.

The Example of Italy

In many countries during the 1920s and 1930s, people tried to find safety in strong leaders who would assert the rights of the nation in a movement sometimes linked to a political trend called fascism. The name "fascism" comes from Benito Mussolini's Fascist Party in Italy. He took power in 1922 and ruled as a virtual dictator. In Germany, Adolf Hitler was another example of a leader who overturned a constitution and promised better times for his people. Strongmen such as Marshal Piłsudski in Poland and Admiral Horthy in Hungary similarly dominated politics in their countries. In Spain, General Franco led an army revolt against the Republican government and took power in 1939.

Western European democratic statesmen wanted to act according to international law, and within the framework of the League of Nations that had been set up in 1920. But they were faced with the ambitions of fascists such as Mussolini, Hitler's attempts to overthrow the peace settlement of 1919, and with a communist regime in Moscow that wanted to tear down the existing social and political order. Try as they might, British and French democratic politicians were unable to stop the slide to war.

KEY DATES

1920 Admiral Horthy becomes regent of Hungary, effectively head of state.

October, 1922 The Blackshirts, followers of Mussolini, march into Rome. The king agrees to make him prime minister and Mussolini creates the first fascist state.

1926 Marshal Józef Piłsudski comes to power in Poland after a military coup.

January 30 1933 Although the Nazi Party does not hold a majority of seats in the Reichstag (parliament), President Hindenburg appoints Adolf Hitler as chancellor of Germany on the advice of conservative politicians.

March 1933 After a fire in its building blamed on communists, the Reichstag passes the enabling act giving Hitler wide-ranging powers to suppress opposition.

1936 Fascist politician Gyula Gömbös comes to power in Hungary.

1936 Francisco Franco leads a military revolt against the Spanish republic. He is helped by Italy and Germany and has taken over the country by 1939.

1 Admiral Horthy became an admiral when Hungary was ruled by the Austro-Hungarian Empire.

2 Francisco Franco in 1930. During the early 1930s he became disenchanted with the elected government and led a revolt in 1936.

3 Benito Mussolini. His party adopted an old Roman symbol, the fasces, a bound bundle of sticks or rods tied around an ax. Hence his party became known as fascists.

4 Józef Piłsudski. He led Polish forces to victory over the Soviet Red Army outside Warsaw in 1920. He is regarded as the father of the interwar Polish republic.

BLITZKRIEG

When German troops flooded across the Polish border on the morning of September 1, 1939, they set off a chain of events that put the world at war for six years.

German vehicles stream through the French countryside in May 1940.

TIMELINE **1940 JANUARY–MAY**

KEY: Politics | Land War | Sea and Air War

February 16 Norway A British destroyer enters neutral waters off Norway to rescue 299 British merchant sailors held by Germans.

April 9 Norway and Denmark Germans invade, defeating Denmark easily; Norway offers more resistance.

January — February — March — April

March 11 Soviet Union Finland and the Soviet Union agree to a peace treaty under which Finland loses 10 percent of its territory; the war has cost 200,000 Soviet dead and 25,000 Finns.

April 14–19 Norway More than 10,000 Allied troops arrive to help Norwegian resistance.

The flat terrain of the Low Countries made the German invasion easier.

In September 1939, Germany attacked an unprepared Poland, which surrendered after heavy losses. The British and French were stunned by the speed of the German conquest. For seven months—the so-called "Phony War"—they prepared for war. Then Hitler also attacked Norway and Denmark.

Huge numbers of French refugees flee the German advance on Paris in June 1940.

KEY DATES

September 1, 1939 Germans invade Poland.

September 3, 1939 Britain and France declare war.

September 8, 1939 Allied Saar Offensive is soon stopped by Germans.

November 1939 Soviets attack Finland.

April 9, 1940 Germans invade neutral Norway.

May 10, 1940 Germany invades Belgium and Holland.

May 7–10, 1940 British Prime Minister Neville Chamberlain resigns. Winston Churchill replaces him.

May 12–14, 1940 Germans invade eastern France.

May 26–June 4, 1940 Operation Dynamo rescues British troops from Dunkirk.

June 14, 1940 German troops enter Paris.

June 22, 1940 France surrenders to Germany.

May

May 7–10 Britain Prime Minister Neville Chamberlain resigns and is replaced by Winston Churchill.

May 10 Low Countries Nazi paratroopers capture Belgium's key fortress and land in Holland; Allied forces advance into Belgium.

May 12–14 France German forces advance through the Ardennes, driving a wedge between the Allied armies in Belgium and France.

May 26 France Operation Dynamo begins to evacuate Allied forces from the port of Dunkirk.

May 28 Belgium King Leopold surrenders as the Allies retreat.

May 31 United States President Franklin D. Roosevelt announces a large-scale arms-building program.

Junkers Ju-87

With its screeching siren, the German Junkers Ju-87 dive-bomber—or Stuka, a short version of its full name—spread terror across Europe during the blitzkrieg years. Stuka pilots dove vertically to only 3,000 feet (915 m) above the ground to deliver their bombs accurately. On the battlefield, the Stukas closely supported panzer divisions by attacking enemy forces that might block an advance. They were known as the "flying artillery of the panzers."

Into the Low Countries

On May 10, 1940, Hitler began his western offensive. With aerial support, panzers (tanks) and infantry poured into Belgium and the Netherlands. The Dutch surrendered on May 14.

British and French forces fighting in Belgium found themselves outflanked by a German tank advance to the south into France. The government

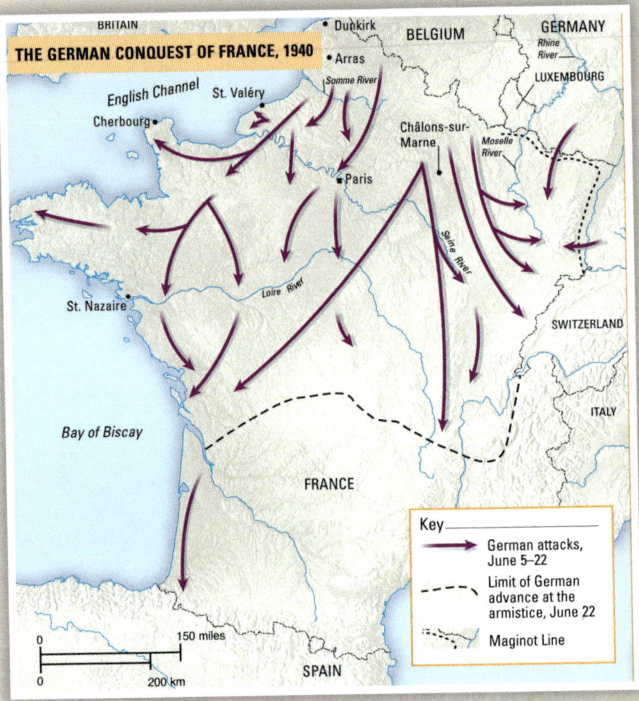

→ The German invasion of central France in June 1940.

TIMELINE 1940 JUNE–AUGUST

KEY: Politics | Land War | Sea and Air War

June

June 4 France
Operation Dynamo ends; the "little ships" rescue 338,226 men from the beaches of Dunkirk.

June 5–10 France
Germans launch Operation Red, the advance on Paris. French morale crumbles, and the army moves south.

June 10 Italy
Italy joins the war on the side of Germany.

June 14 France
Germans enter Paris unopposed.

June 16–24 France A peace treaty gives Germany control of two-thirds of France; the south is under a puppet French government based at Vichy.

June 30 Channel Islands
German troops invade; the islands are the only British home territory occupied during the war.

July

Stuka dive-bombers were an essential part of the German tactic of blitzkrieg, or lightning war.

of the new prime minister, Winston Churchill, ordered the British Expeditionary Force to retreat to the port of Dunkirk, from where it was evacuated by the Royal Navy (see right), but more than 1.2 million Allied soldiers were captured. Belgium surrendered on May 28.

On to Paris

The Germans gathered two million troops for an advance on Paris. The city fell without violence on June 14. The French laid down their arms on June 22.

Scandinavia

The Allies pulled out of Norway following the invasion of the Low Countries and France. Germany was now in control of much of northern Europe.

"Little Ships"

The docks at Dunkirk were full, so the navy called for volunteers to help rescue the army from the beaches. A fleet of "little ships"—commercial or leisure craft—sailed across the English Channel. They rescued some 30,000 men each day in the face of air attack and ferried them to larger vessels offshore. The evacuation ensured the survival of the British army—and perhaps of Britain.

Allied sailors and troops in a lifeboat after their ship was bombed and sunk off Dunkirk.

July 1 Atlantic Ocean U-boats begin to inflict heavy losses on Allied convoys; the "Happy Time" lasts until October.

July 3 Algeria Fearing French ships in Algeria will be used by Germans, British attack them and disarm French naval forces in Alexandria, Egypt.

July 10 Britain The Battle of Britain begins when Goering orders attacks on Allied shipping and ports in the English Channel.

July 21 Eastern Front Soviets take over Lithuania, Latvia, and Estonia.

August

August 24–25 Britain The Luftwaffe inflicts serious damage on RAF bases; British air defenses are close to breaking point.

August 26–29 Germany The RAF launches night raids on Berlin and other cities; the Germans bomb London in revenge.

Tank Warfare

Tanks were the armored spearhead of land warfare during World War II.

In World War I, any soldiers in open ground on the battlefield were vulnerable to machine-gun fire. This made it very difficult for them to advance against enemy positions. The war, especially on the Western Front, became bogged down and defenders managed to stop almost all offensives. Late in the war, however, the Allies used what the British called tanks—vehicles with armor plating. Tanks did not move quickly, but they had caterpillar tracks that enabled them to move across all types of terrain.

1

Blitzkrieg

By 1939 tanks had developed. Just as important as the technology was a new type of military principle adopted by the German Army. Tanks were to be used to break through front lines and then carry on deep into enemy territory. The Germans called this way of fighting *Blitzkrieg* ("lightning war"). Blitzkrieg led to many important German victories early in World War II, in Western Europe, North Africa, and the Soviet Union.

As the war went on, tanks became bigger and carried heavier guns. The German Mark II tank of 1939 weighed 8.9 tons (7.9 metric tons) and carried a 20 mm gun. The Soviet JSII tank of 1945 weighed 51 tons (45 metric tons) and carried a 122 mm gun. In the end, the German Army was overwhelmed by the massive combined tank forces of the Allies.

2

KEY DATES

1916 The British Army uses the first tanks in the Battle of the Somme.

August 1918 Britain and France use tanks in mass attacks on German positions.

1919 British Army officer Colonel J. F. C. Fuller comes up with an idea for using tanks to break through enemy defenses.

1935 The German Army forms three tank divisions.

July 1941 German forces invading the Soviet Union are surprised by the power of the Russian T-34 tank. Over 80,000 T-34s were built.

October 1942 The M4 Sherman tank enters the combat. Over 49,000 Sherman tanks were eventually produced. It became the backbone of the armored forces of the Western Allies.

July 1943 Battle of Kursk, the largest tank battle of World War II. Almost 5,000 Red Army tanks take on 2,500 German tanks. The Soviet Union wins a decisive victory.

January 1945 The Red Army deploys 4,500 tanks in its invasion of Germany.

1 A huge King Tiger tank used in the defense of Budapest in 1945. This was the largest tank the Germans produced.

2 Infantry hitch a ride on Soviet tanks during the Battle of Kursk, in which the Red Army defeated the major German offensive.

3 A small Mark II German tank used early in World War II. Mark IIs were used in Poland and Western Europe in 1939–40.

4 Tank destroyers were developed to fight the tanks. This Allied tank destroyer has an anti-tank gun on a Sherman tank chassis.

5 German tanks were grouped in special armored divisions that could break through enemy lines.

Battle of Britain

With the defeat of France and the Low Countries in 1940, Britain stood alone in Europe against the Nazi threat. It faced an enemy that was poised to attack its shores.

British pilots run to their planes. The RAF used radar to respond swiftly to any enemy threat.

TIMELINE 1940 SEPTEMBER–DECEMBER

KEY: Politics | Land War | Sea and Air War

September

September 7 Britain Full-scale bombing raids on London—the "Blitz"—begins; the city is bombed for 57 consecutive days.

September 13-18 Egypt Italians invade British-controlled Egypt.

September 20-22 Atlantic Ocean German U-boats sink 12 Allied ships in "wolf pack" operations; a pack gathers 15 to 20 U-boats for an attack on a convoy.

September 27 Germany Germany, Italy, and Japan agree to the Tripartite Pact; they will all attack any state that declares war on any of the three of them.

October

October 28 Greece Italian troops invade Greece from Albania but meet stiff resistance.

St. Paul's Cathedral rises above smoke after a bombing raid in 1940.

By the summer of 1940, the future looked bleak for the Allies. Hitler ordered the invasion of Britain, code-named Operation Sealion. The invasion faced a major obstacle: the English Channel. In order for German forces to cross it safely, it was vital to defeat the Royal Air Force (RAF).

Battle of Britain

The two air forces were finely balanced in June 1940, but the RAF did have one advantage. The Chain Home Radar System detected enemy

KEY DATES

July 10, 1940 The Luftwaffe attack Allied shipping and ports in the English Channel, beginning the Battle of Britain.

July 16, 1940 Hitler plans Operation Sealion, the invasion of Britain, for August 15.

August 24, 1940 German bombs are dropped on London.

August 25, 1940 Retaliatory bombing of Berlin.

September 7, 1940 Bombing of London (the "Blitz") begins.

September 15, 1940 Climax of the Battle of Britain.

September 17, 1940 Hitler postpones Operation Sealion.

May 10-11, 1941 507 German bombers attack London in the largest raid of the Blitz.

Spitfires fly in tandem. The British fighters were renowned for their speed and handling.

November

November 5 United States
President Franklin D. Roosevelt is elected for an unprecedented third term.

November 11-12 Mediterranean
At the Battle of Taranto, British aircraft and cruisers devastate the Italian fleet.

November 14 Britain
A nighttime bombing raid on the city of Coventry kills 500 civilians and leaves thousands more homeless.

December

December 9-11 Egypt
British begin the first offensive in North Africa; some 34,000 Italians are taken prisoner as they retreat rapidly from Egypt.

Radar

The development of radar was a triumph for British science. In 1935, there were worries that Germany was developing a "death ray." Scientists Robert Watson-Watt and Arnold Wilkins showed in experiments that radio waves could not create a death ray, but that they could detect incoming aircraft. The government immediately invested. By 1938 five radar stations were in place. Finally, the RAF created a method of using radar to control air defense.

➔ British and German air bases during the Battle of Britain.

THE BATTLE OF BRITAIN, 1940

German bomber stations
German HQ
RAF fighter airfield
Radar station
RAF HQ
Limits of fighter command groups
German fighter limits

Newcastle
FIGHTER COMMAND GROUP 13
Hull
Liverpool
Manchester
Nottingham
FIGHTER COMMAND GROUP 12
Norwich
BRITAIN
Cardiff
FIGHTER COMMAND GROUP 11
London
FIGHTER COMMAND GROUP 10
Southampton
Plymouth
English Channel
Cherbourg
BELGIUM
Paris
FRANCE
Range of low-level radar
Range of high-level radar
0 100 miles
0 200 km

aircraft as they crossed the English Channel.

From late June until August 12, 1940, RAF and Luftwaffe fighter planes fought dogfights above the Channel. Both sides suffered heavy losses, but British resistance eventually forced Hitler to delay Operation Sealion. The Battle of Britain was a victory for the RAF and its pilots, whom Churchill named "the Few."

➔ The Chain Home Radar installation at Polling in Sussex.

Bombing Campaign

After German bombers accidentally bombed London, Churchill authorized a bombing raid on Berlin. Hitler was

TIMELINE **1940 JANUARY–APRIL**

KEY: Politics | Land War | Sea and Air War

January

January 2 United States President Roosevelt announces a ship-building program to support Allied Atlantic convoys.

February

February 3 Atlantic Ocean German battle cruisers begin a campaign against Allied merchant ships; they sink 22 vessels before returning to base on March 22.

February 14 North Africa German general Erwin Rommel's skilled Afrika Korps arrives at Tripoli, Libya, to help the Italians.

enraged. In turn, he ordered the bombing of London and Britain's major cities. However, the need to defend Germany's cities against possible air raids meant that the Luftwaffe had to leave aircraft at home and had fewer to fight the British.

Britain was saved from an imminent invasion but the destruction continued. In early September 1940, German bombers began full-scale raids on London and other cities. The capital was bombed for 57 consecutive days. This "Blitz" against civilian and industrial targets continued well into 1944. Its peak passed by May 1941, however, when Germany pulled aircraft east to invade the Soviet Union. Despite the huge destruction it caused, the Blitz failed to crush Britain industry or to destroy the morale of its people.

Air Raids

From September 1940, Londoners got used to almost nightly air raids. Many Londoners slept in cellars, subway stations, or purpose-built air-raid shelters. A "blackout" was put into practice, but German pilots navigated by features such as rivers, so it had little effect. By the end of the Blitz in May 1941, about 40,000 people had died in the raids and huge amounts of property in London and other cities had been destroyed.

Onlookers view a bomb crater in front of the Bank of England, London, in January 1941.

March

April

March 11 United States
President Roosevelt signs the Lend-Lease Act, which allows Britain to get war supplies without paying immediately.

March 28-29 Mediterranean
Italian and British fleets clash in the Aegean Sea. Five Italian ships are sunk and 3,000 men are killed for the loss of only one British aircraft.

April 6-15 Yugoslavia
German, Italian, and Hungarian forces invade Yugoslavia.

April 17 Yugoslavia
Yugoslavia surrenders but guerrilla forces—partisans—continue a resistance campaign.

April 18-21 Greece
British troops sent to help Greeks are forced back to the southern coast by German troops and are evacuated to Crete.

Winston Churchill

Prime minister from May 1940, Churchill proved to be an inspiring war leader.

Winston Churchill was seen as something of a maverick in the 1930s. He had been a member of two different political parties and some of his decisions when in office during World War I, especially the decision to attack Turkish positions on Gallipoli, had been disastrous. In the 1930s, he had expressed vigorous opposition to the government's policy of "appeasing" Germany by allowing Hitler a free hand in Czechoslovakia. Churchill was recognized as having been right about Hitler when World War II broke out.

The War Years

In 1940, when Hitler was attacking Western Europe, Winston Churchill replaced Neville Chamberlain as prime minister. He galvanized Britain during the dark days of summer 1940, when it seemed that Germany would invade. His speeches and his radio broadcasts expressed confidence in the ability of the country to resist the enemy, and kept up civilian morale during the German bombing of London and other cities.

Churchill forged a good relationship with Franklin D. Roosevelt even before the United States entered the war. American aid flowed into Britain well before the Japanese attack on the U.S. fleet in Pearl Harbor in December 1941. Churchill was determined to keep the British Empire intact and many of his policies later in the war were based on this rather than on the quickest way to defeat Nazi Germany.

KEY DATES

November 30, 1874 Winston Churchill is born into an aristocratic family in the U.K. His mother was American, the daughter of a U.S. businessman.

September 2, 1898 Churchill takes part in a cavalry charge as a member of the 21st Lancers at the Battle of Omdurman.

May 31, 1904 Now a member of Parliament, Churchill defects from the Conservative Party to the Liberals.

1911 Churchill becomes First Lord of the Admiralty, head of the Royal Navy.

November 1915 Churchill resigns after the landing of troops on the Gallipoli peninsula in Turkey is a disaster.

November 1934 Churchill speaks against the ambitions of Hitler and Nazi Germany in a radio broadcast.

September 3, 1939 World War II breaks out. Churchill is reappointed as First Lord of the Admiralty.

May 10, 1940 Churchill is elected prime minister of the United Kingdom.

January 24, 1965 Churchill dies and is later given a state funeral.

1 Churchill as a young officer, wearing the uniform of the 4th Queen's Own Hussars in 1895 at the British Army base of Aldershot.

2 Churchill at the Potsdam Conference with U.S. President Harry Truman (center) in July 1945, after the defeat of Germany.

3 Churchill in 1941, while on a visit to Canada where he met President Roosevelt on board the battleship *Prince of Wales*.

4 Prime Minister Churchill firing a British automatic weapon, the Sten submachine gun, in Kent, England, in 1941.

The Battle of the Atlantic

The Battle of the Atlantic began the day Britain declared war on Nazi Germany and ended on May 7, 1945. It was the longest and arguably most important battle of the war.

A British destroyer escorts merchant ships traveling from the United States to Britain in April 1940.

TIMELINE **1941 MAY–AUGUST**

KEY: Politics | Land War | Sea and Air War

May — June

May 3–19 Ethiopia
The Battle of Amba Alagi in northern Ethiopia ends with Italian surrender to the British.

May 10 Britain
Rudolph Hess, deputy leader of the Nazis, flies secretly to Scotland to make a peace deal with the British; he is imprisoned.

May 10–11 Britain
In the largest raid of the Blitz, 507 bombers attack London.

May 20–22 Crete
Some 23,000 German troops land. They are attacked by British, New Zealand, and Australian troops, but gain a foothold.

May 28–31 Crete
The Germans take Crete. Losses are similar on both German and British sides.

The German battleship *Bismarck* fires at HMS *Hood* in the Battle of Denmark Strait.

At the start of World War II, Britain's Royal Navy was the largest in the world. The much smaller German Navy, the Kriegsmarine, could not hope to take on the British fleet. Instead, the Germans planned to sink merchant vessels carrying supplies to Britain, mainly from North America. The Germans' key weapon was the U-boat (short for *Unterseeboot*, the German word for submarine). Hunting in "wolf packs," the U-boats preyed on undefended merchant vessels. The task was so easy the U-boat crews called the early part of the war the "Happy Time."

German U-boat technicians prepare torpedoes in 1941.

KEY DATES

September 3, 1939 German *U-30* sinks British passenger liner *Athenia*.

December 13, 1939 Battle of River Plate in neutral Uruguay.

May 1941 Battle of Denmark Strait results in the destruction of the most powerful German battleship, *Bismarck*.

August 1941 Start of the Arctic convoys aiding the Soviet Union.

December 11, 1941 United States enters the war.

July 1942 United States adopts convoy system after heavy merchantman losses.

December 1942 HMS *Audacity*, a new generation of small escort carriers, is sunk.

November 12, 1944 Pride of the German Navy, the *Tirpitz*, finally destroyed.

May 1945 The German Navy surrenders.

June 15–17 North Africa
The British launch Operation Battle-axe to relieve troops trapped by the Afrika Korps in the Libyan port of Tobruk. They stop after heavy tank losses.

June 22 Soviet Union
Germany launches Operation Barbarossa to invade the Soviet Union; German air attacks quickly destroy 1,800 Soviet aircraft on the ground.

July

July 4 Yugoslavia
Joseph Broz, known as "Tito," emerges as leader of Yugoslav partisans.

July 16 Soviet Union
Around 300,000 Red Army troops and 3,200 tanks are trapped near the city of Smolensk.

July 31 Germany
Reinhard Heydrich, head of the German SS secret police, ordered to plan extermination of Europe's Jews: the "Final Solution."

August

U-boat Tactics

Initially U-boats hunted alone, usually attacking targets in daylight when submerged. As more U-boats were built, they hunted in "wolf packs" of 15 to 20 vessels that attacked together at night. The tactic began in fall 1940 and was successful until 1943. Britain's initial lack of escort vessels meant that there was little risk to the U-boats. Later, faster escorts, sonar equipment, and increased air power doomed the wolf packs to defeat.

The Convoy System

Britain adopted a convoy system in which groups of merchant ships could be escorted by warships. However, Britain lacked convoy escort ships, and its vessels were ineffective at hunting U-boats. By the end of 1940, Britain seemed close to losing the Battle of the Atlantic. By December 1940, the British had lost 20 percent of their merchant fleet. In contrast, the Germans had lost just six U-boats.

Britain Fights Back

The Allies slowly discovered better ways to defeat the German threat. Long-range aircraft provided air cover, while mines and other innovations made it easier to destroy U-boats. In May 1941, Germany's most powerful battleship, *Bismarck*, was damaged in the Battle of Denmark Strait and was then hunted down and destroyed. It was a huge boost to British morale.

→ U-boats spent long periods on the surface, but went underwater when they attacked in daylight.

TIMELINE **1941 SEPTEMBER–DECEMBER**

KEY: Politics | Land War | Sea and Air War

September

September 3 Poland
Experiments to kill Jewish prisoners in gas chambers are carried out in Auschwitz camp.

September 4 Atlantic Ocean
A U-boat mistakes the U.S. destroyer *Greer* for a British vessel and attacks it; U.S. warships are ordered to "shoot on sight" any U-boats they see.

September 19 Soviet Union
German troops take Kiev.

September 30 Soviet Union
The Germans begin Operation Typhoon, a full-scale attack on Moscow.

October

Survivors from a sinking ship row to a German U-boat to be taken prisoner.

The Enigma Code

Enigma was used by the Germans to transmit complex codes that changed daily. British intelligence even built one of the first-ever computers, Colossus, to help crack the code. A breakthrough came in March 1941, when an Enigma machine was found on a captured U-boat. It allowed the British to decipher information that proved vital to the Allied victory.

Help from the United States

After the United States entered the war in December 1941, it suffered heavy losses of merchant shipping as U-boats patrolled the East Coast. The Germans referred to early 1942 as a second "Happy Time." It was shortlived, however. As Allied antisubmarine tactics and technology improved, they were able to destroy the U-boats in large numbers. As German losses mounted, the U-boats were withdrawn to France, where they were kept in port. After the Allied invasion of France in June 1944, many of the submarines were destroyed. The Germans had effectively lost the Battle of the Atlantic.

Enigma had a system of rotors that turned messages into code.

November

December

November 18–26 North Africa
British relieve Tobruk despite heavy losses; Rommel retreats.

December 7 Hawaii
Japanese aircraft attack the U.S. fleet at Pearl Harbor, killing 2,000 people and destroying six battleships.

December 8 Soviet Union
Adolf Hitler halts the advance on Moscow for the winter; the German panzers cannot operate in the freezing temperatures.

December 11 United States
Germany and Italy declare war on the United States, which declares war on them in return.

December 18–19 Egypt
Italian midget submarines, each with two operators, sink two British battleships in Alexandria harbor, Egypt.

Operation Barbarossa

Operation Barbarossa was the most ambitious campaign of World War II. Hitler invaded the Soviet Union to gain *lebensraum* ("living space") for the German people.

German Mark III panzers advance on the Eastern Front.

TIMELINE **1942 JANUARY–APRIL**

KEY:  **Politics** **Land War** **Sea and Air War**

January

January 5 Soviet Union
Stalin's troops counterattack; their initial success halts as the Germans set up well-defended areas known as "hedgehogs."

January 13 Atlantic Ocean
U-boats attack shipping off the East Coast of the United States.

January 16–19 Germany
Hitler sacks more than 30 senior generals because they want to withdraw in the face of Soviet attacks on the Eastern Front.

January 20 Germany
The "FInal Solution"—the extermination of Europe's Jews—becomes key to Nazi war plans at the Wannsee Conference in Berlin.

February

German progress was fast along the Soviet front.

KEY DATES

Summer 1940 German High Command plans Operation Barbarossa.

Spring 1941 Soviet divisions mass along western border.

June 22, 1941 German artillery opens fire on Soviet troops.

Late June 1941 Minsk is captured.

Mid-July 1941 Smolensk is captured

July 3, 1941 Stalin launches his "scorched earth" policy; troops destroy anything that could fall into German hands.

August 21, 1941 Hitler orders his forces to advance through Ukraine.

September 19, 1941 Kiev falls to the Germans.

The German High Command began planning Operation Barbarossa in summer 1940, despite the nonaggression pact signed with the Soviets in 1939. Hitler claimed that Stalin was preparing to attack Germany. Stalin did have troops on his western borders, but they were mainly defensive. Germany gathered one of the largest invasion forces ever assembled.

German artillery opens fire on the Eastern Front in the early hours of June 22, 1941.

February 11-12 North Sea The Channel Dash sees German battle cruisers speed to the North Sea from France before the British can stop them.

February 14 Singapore The British based at Singapore surrender to the Japanese.

February 27-29 Java Sea The Japanese inflict heavy losses on Allied fleet.

March

March 28-29 France British commandos attack the St. Nazaire dry dock, used by the Germans to repair warships, but 144 men are killed in the raid and many more are captured.

April

April 9 Philippines U.S. and Philippine forces in the Philippines surrender to the Japanese. Many die on a 65-mile (105 km) forced march into captivity.

April 18 Japan In a raid led by James Doolittle, 16 U.S. B-25 bombers launched from an aircraft carrier attack Tokyo; Japan's leaders decide to seek a battle to destroy U.S. naval power in the Pacific.

Soviet Factories Move East

Factories in the western Soviet Union were threatened by the German advance in fall of 1941. So entire factories were taken down, put onto railroad cars, and moved east to the safety of the Ural Mountains. Up to 25 million workers also moved. They went straight back to work in the new factories. Even in the freezing winter temperatures, Soviet production never stopped.

The offensive had three massive thrusts: toward Leningrad (now called St. Petersburg); toward Kiev, the capital of Ukraine; and toward Smolensk, west of Moscow. Despite the warning signs, Stalin and his generals were taken by surprise when German artillery opened fire along the Soviet border at 3:30 a.m. on June 22, 1941. The invasion of the Soviet Union had begun.

The Advance Slows

In the first weeks the invasion was unstoppable. German panzers advanced far into the Soviet Union. However, by mid-July the advance had slowed down. Muddy roads delayed German supplies, and the advancing troops could not rely on finding food or fuel. Stalin had ordered

➔ A T-34 rolls off the production line in a factory in a city named "Tankograd."

TIMELINE **1942 MAY–AUGUST**

KEY: Politics | Land War | Sea and Air War

May

May 26–31 North Africa The Battle of Gazala. Rommel attacks the British, but his tanks suffer serious fuel problems until the Italians provide supplies on May 31.

May 31 Germany Britain launches its first "1,000 bomber raid" on Cologne; 59,000 people are left homeless.

June

June 4 Pacific Ocean U.S. naval forces win a decisive victory over the Japanese at the Battle of Midway.

June 10–13 North Africa Rommel's way to Tobruk is open as British withdraw after the Battle of Gazala.

June 21 North Africa Rommel captures Tobruk.

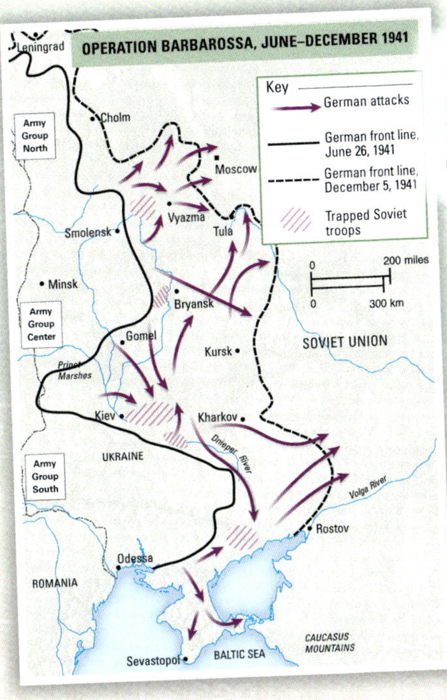

German advances made significant gains in the first six months of the invasion.

a "scorched earth" policy, which meant that crops, fuel, and any other potentially useful resources were destroyed by the retreating Soviets.

Kiev Falls

Despite opposition from his High Command, Hitler ordered his troops to advance to Kiev. On September 15, two panzer groups encircled the city. It fell on September 19, 1941, in spite of Stalin's order that it should be defended at all costs. Hitler hailed the fall of Kiev as "the greatest battle in world history." Many of his commanders, however, saw it as a strategic error that distracted them from their primary target: the advance on Moscow.

The Siege of Leningrad

As German troops closed in on Leningrad in fall 1941, some 700,000 of its three million inhabitants fled. Rationing began for the remainder, but people began to die of starvation as supply routes were cut off. In January 1942, however, Lake Ladoga froze and it became possible to drive trucks across it. The Soviets built a road 20 miles (32 km) long across the ice, which became known as the "Road of Life." The siege was broken in January 1944 after the Germans were forced to retreat.

July

August

June 28 Soviet Union
The Germans launch summer offensive, Operation Blue, into southern Russia to capture oil fields in the Caucasus.

July 4–10 Soviet Union
After a two-month siege, the Germans capture the port of Sevastopol and about 90,000 Red Army troops.

August 7 Guadalcanal
U.S. Marines land on Guadalcanal and face fierce resistance from the Japanese.

August 19 France
A combined Canadian, British, and American force attacks the port of Dieppe. It is a disaster, with most men killed.

August 23 Soviet Union
A raid by 600 German bombers on Stalingrad kills thousands.

Joseph Stalin

A committed revolutionary in his youth, Stalin ruled the Soviet Union for almost 30 years.

Stalin means "steel," or "man of iron." In 1912 the radical communist Joseph Jughashvili adopted it as his name. In 1922, Joseph Stalin succeeded Vladimir Lenin as leader of the Russian Bolshevik Party and maintained power in a ruthless dictatorship in which millions of people died. Isolated by the western European democracies, Stalin came to an agreement with Hitler in 1939, by which both countries invaded and divided up Poland. Stalin went on to make an unsuccessful attack on Finland in late-1939.

1

Victory Over Germany

In 1941, Stalin refused to believe advice that Germany was planning to attack the Soviet Union. As a result, the Soviet Union suffered catastrophic losses in the first months of Operation Barbarossa from June 1941. During this period Stalin seems to have suffered a breakdown for a short period, but he recovered and led the resistance to the invaders, staying in Moscow even when German troops were just a few miles from the capital.

Unlike Hitler, Stalin rarely tried to interfere in battlefield decisions. He was prepared to defer to the advice of his senior generals such as Marshal Zhukov. Soviet armies gradually overcame the German war machine and Stalin occupied much of eastern and central Europe, putting it under the effective control of local Soviet-backed Communist parties.

2

KEY DATES

November 18, 1878 The man later known as Joseph Stalin is born in Gori, a town in what is now Georgia. His father is a shoemaker.

May 1901 Stalin organizes a demonstration against the Russian authorities in Tiflis in Georgia

1917 Stalin becomes editor of the Bolshevik Party's newspaper, *Pravda* ("Truth").

1920 Stalin is a commander in a Red Army invasion of Poland that is defeated.

1929 Stalin announces the state ownership of agriculture, which leads to a disastrous famine.

1937 The period of the "Great Purge." Stalin executes many leading members of the Bolshevik Party and thousands of ordinary Russians.

June 1941 Germany invades the Soviet Union in Operation Barbarossa. Stalin declares himself head of the armed forces.

October 16, 1952 Stalin dies.

1 Stalin, aged 23. He took part in violent attacks on the Tsarist state that ruled Russia, and also wrote poetry.

2 A secret police mugshot of Stalin in 1911, following his arrest for "revolutionary activities." It was the second time he had been arrested, the first being in 1908.

3 Stalin (left) and German Foreign Minister von Ribbentrop in 1939, sealing the secret deal that would lead both nations to invade Poland.

4 Stalin (seated, right) at the Potsdam Conference in 1945. With him are U.S. President Harry Truman (seated, center) and British Prime Minister Clement Attlee (seated, left).

North Africa

The war in the North African deserts saw Axis and Allied troops fight for two years to control the region and gain access to the oil fields of the Middle East.

British troops defend the Gazala Line. They fire a 25-pounder gun, one of the best field guns of the war.

TIMELINE **1942 SEPTEMBER–DECEMBER**

KEY: Pacific | Europe and North Africa | Sea and Air War

September

September 2 Poland
The Nazis "clear" the Jewish Warsaw Ghetto; more than 50,000 Jews are killed.

October

October 23 North Africa
The Second Battle of El Alamein begins in Egypt.

THE AXIS ADVANCE IN NORTH AFRICA, JANUARY–JULY 1942

Key
Axis attacks
British positions

Mediterranean Sea
Benghazi (January 29)
Barce
Derna
Gazala line (May 26)
Gazala
Tobruk (June 21)
Msus (January 25)
"The Cauldron"
Fort Capuzzo
Bardia
Sidi Barrani
Haifaya
Buq Buq
Mersa Matruh
LIBYA
Qattara Depression
El Alamein (June 30)
El Agheila
0 100 miles

↑ Axis troops made significant advances in Africa between January and July 1942.

Fighting in Africa began in 1940. Italian dictator Benito Mussolini hoped to create an empire there. British troops fought back the Italians, but the advantage swung back to the Axis with the arrival of the German Afrika Korps under General Erwin Rommel in early 1941.

KEY DATES

January 1942 Germans prepare for new offensive.

July 1, 1942 1st Battle of El Alamein starts as Rommel attacks Allied troops.

July 22, 1942 Rommel calls off offensive.

August 1942 Churchill makes Montgomery commander of the 8th Army.

August 30, 1942 Battle of Alam Halfa.

October 23, 1942 2nd Battle of El Alamein.

November 8, 1942 Operation Torch begins.

February 19–25, 1943 Battle of Kasserine Pass. U.S. troops are defeated.

March 26, 1943 Allied troops break through behind Mareth Line.

May 13, 1943 Axis forces surrender in North Africa.

← The First Battle of El Alamein halted Rommel's advance, but with 13,000 casualties.

November 19 Soviet Union
General Georgi Zhukov launches an attack to relieve Stalingrad; the pincer movement traps the Germans fighting in the city and the German front collapses.

November

December

November 2–24 North Africa
The Second Battle of El Alamein. Rommel is forced to retreat; it is the first major defeat suffered by German forces during the war.

December 19 Soviet Union
A German counterattack fails to rescue the Sixth Army trapped in Stalingrad, where conditions are deteriorating and food is short.

Erwin Rommel

Commonwealth and British soldiers in North Africa came to see Rommel as some kind of military genius during the first months of 1942. He seemed able to conjure victory out of certain defeat. Only when Rommel was defeated at Alam Halfa and El Alamein in autumn 1942 was the myth finally exploded.

➔ Captured German soldiers in the desert wait to be taken to a prisoner-of-war camp

Rommel broke through the Allied lines at Gazala, captured the port of Tobruk, and headed east toward Egypt. The Allies retreated to a defensive line at the village of El Alamein. There, on October 23, 1942, some 195,000 Allied troops under Field Marshal Bernard Montgomery clashed with 105,000 Axis soldiers.

Battles of El Alamein

Fighting continued through November until, after some three weeks, Rommel gave up. He retreated

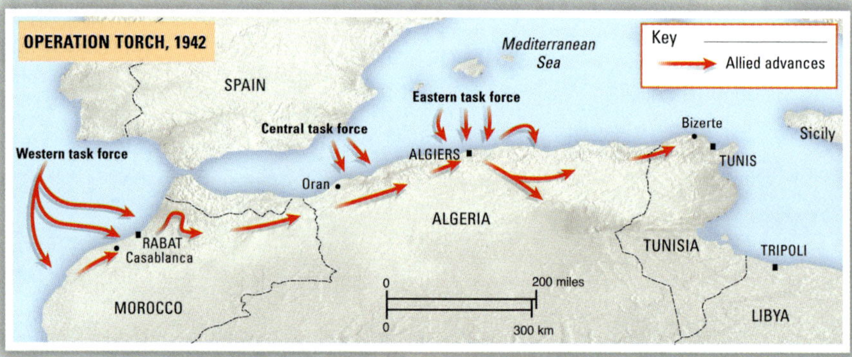

➔ Operation Torch was the first U.S. campaign of the war in the west.

TIMELINE 1943 JANUARY–APRIL

KEY: Pacific | Europe and North Africa | Sea and Air War

January

January 18 Poland
Jewish fighters in the Warsaw Ghetto begin attacking German troops.

January 31 Guadalcanal
U.S. troops finally capture the island of Guadalcanal in the Pacific after six months' fighting.

February

February 2 Soviet Union
The Siege of Stalingrad ends when 93,000 German troops surrender.

February 14–22 North Africa
Inexperienced U.S. troops suffer heavy losses in the Battle of Kasserine Pass.

February 16 Germany
Students demonstrate against Hitler's regime in Munich; the leaders are executed.

February 18 Burma
British Chindits parachute behind Japanese lines for a six-week mission to raid enemy supply lines.

U.S. troops bring a gun ashore in the joint U.S.-British invasion of northwest Africa.

Afrika Korps

Rommel's Afrika Korps staged a daring offensive in early 1942 with a small but well-equipped force that pushed the British back into Egypt. But by summer 1942, the Korps needed supplies and was undermanned. Hitler refused requests for more resources. At El Alamein, Panzer Group Afrika was forced into a long retreat by the better-supplied British Eighth Army. Rommel was recalled from Africa on March 6, 1943. The decimated Axis forces in North Africa surrendered on May 13.

more than 1,000 miles (1,600 km) back into Tunisia. El Alamein was a decisive defeat. The Germans were unable to regain their position in North Africa.

Operation Torch

At the same time, the United States joined the war in North Africa. U.S. troops landed in Morocco to join Operation Torch to rid the region of Axis forces. After heavy fighting, the Allies threatened to encircle the Germans, who retreated. Rommel returned to Germany and after a final Allied push, Axis forces in North Africa surrendered.

In North Africa the Axis lost more than a million troops for no territorial gain. The losses were a serious blow to Hitler's war effort.

March

March 14 Soviet Union German forces destroy the Soviet Third Tank Army, forcing Soviets to abandon newly won territory on the Eastern Front.

March 15 Soviet Union The Germans launch Operation Citadel, a plan to destroy Red Army troops near the city of Kursk.

April

April 12 Soviet Union The Germans find a mass grave in Katyn Forest containing the bodies of 10,000 Polish army officers executed by the Soviet secret police in 1939.

April 17 Germany U.S. bombers attack the German city of Bremen.

Struggle for Malta

The island of Malta played a pivotal role in the struggle for Mediterranean supremacy.

Malta lies some 50 miles (80 km) south of the Italian island of Sicily. It had been part of the British Empire since the early 19th century and after Italy declared war in 1940 it became a key strategic island in the Mediterranean and North African campaigns. Italian forces based in North Africa (Italy had taken over Libya early in the 20th century) attacked British forces in Egypt and relied on resupply by sea. British submarines based on Malta threatened these Italian supply ships. The importance of Malta grew when German forces were sent to North Africa in 1941 and the campaigns there grew in scale and intensity.

1

Heavy Losses

Malta was bombed by Italian and German aircraft but was never taken by Axis forces, although attempts to keep Malta supplied and fighting led to losses for the Royal Navy. Of 16 merchant vessels that set out in convoy "Pedestal" in August 1942, only five reached Malta. One British aircraft carrier and two cruisers escorting the convoy were also sunk. The sacrifice was felt to be worthwhile, as holding Malta starved the Germans of access to fuel they needed for their tanks in North Africa. Malta was awarded the George Cross in April 1942, the highest British civilian medal and the equivalent of the military Victoria Cross, because of the bravery of its people.

2

KEY DATES

1814 Malta formally becomes part of the British Empire at the Congress of Vienna.

1937 The headquarters of the Royal Navy Mediterranean fleet is moved from Malta because it is too close to Italian airfields.

June 10, 1940 Italy declares war on Great Britain. Fifty five Italian bombers attack Malta that day.

July-December 1941 Aircraft and submarines based on Malta sink 60 percent of Axis supplies intended for North Africa.

March 1942 Spitfire fighter aircraft are sent to Malta to bolster the air defences.

April 1942 Hitler approves Operation Hercules, a plan to land paratroops on Malta after intense aerial attack. The plan is never activated.

January 1943 It is estimated that British U-class submarines have sunk 600,000 tons of Axis merchant shipping during the siege of Malta. However, 38 Royal Navy submarines were lost.

1 A British U-Class submarine returns to its base in Malta. Malta-based submarines were critical in cutting Axis supply routes.

2 The results of bombing raids on Valletta, the main port and city of Malta. The bombing began the day Italy entered the war.

3 The armed trawler HMS *Coral*, a ship used for reconnaissance and anti-submarine operations, in a damaged dry dock in Valletta.

4 An Italian Savoia-Marchetti bomber. Such aircraft returned to attack the island again and again during the period from 1940 to 1943.

5 A British task force escorting the Pedestal convoy toward the island. The convoy was subject to ceaseless attack.

Sicily and Italy

In 1943, the Allies began a campaign to invade Europe from the south by targeting Sicily. They hoped that occupying the island would knock Italy out of the war.

An American soldier leads a convoy of German prisoners in Sicily, 1944.

TIMELINE **1943 MAY–AUGUST**

KEY: Pacific | Europe and North Africa | Sea and Air War

May

May 13 North Africa
Axis forces surrender to the Allies; 620,000 Axis casualties and prisoners had been lost in the campaign.

May 16 Poland
Warsaw Ghetto uprising ends; it has been harshly repressed by the Germans.

May 16–17 Germany The Dambusters Raid. The British use "bouncing bombs" to destroy dams in Germany's industrial Ruhr region.

June

June 10 Germany
Operation Pointblank. British and U.S. bombers begin a year-long series of attacks on German industry.

July

July 5 Soviet Union
The Battle of Kursk is the largest tank battle in history; the Germans make little progress against the Soviets.

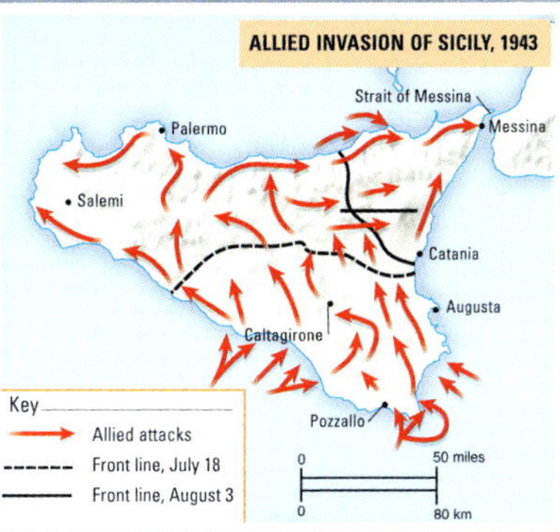

Allied troops landed on the south side of Sicily and then pushed north.

After the conquest of North Africa, the Allies planned an attack on Sicily to provide a base for a move to the Italian mainland. It would also divert as many Germans as possible from northwest Europe. The invasion of Sicily, code-named Operation Husky, was an amphibious (land and sea) assault. For almost a month, the Allies dropped thousands of tons of bombs on airfields, ports, bridges, rail links, and supply depots. British and U.S. paratroopers and glider-borne

KEY DATES

January 1943 Allied leaders decide to capture Sicily before invading Italy.

April/May 1943 Operation Mincemeat fools Hitler into diverting defenders to Greece and Sardinia.

July 10, 1943 Operation Husky begins.

July 25, 1943 Mussolini fired.

September 3, 1943 Italians sign armistice with the Allies.

September 9, 1943 Allied troops land in southern Italy.

September 16, 1943 German troops withdraw north.

May 11–18, 1944 Allies break through the Gustav Line at Monte Cassino.

June 5, 1944 U.S. troops enter Rome.

April 29, 1945 German forces in northern Italy surrender.

British troops wade ashore during the Allied invasion of Sicily, 1943.

July 12–13 Soviet Union The Soviets narrowly defeat the Germans at Kursk. The battle leaves 500,000 casualties dead, injured, or missing.

July 25 Italy The king of Italy sacks Benito Mussolini. The new leader, Pietro Badoglio, hopes that the Allies will occupy Italy before it falls under German control.

August

July 10 Sicily Operation Husky. U.S. and British troops invade.

July 24–August 2 Germany The British bomb Hamburg, killing around 50,000 civilians and leaving some 800,000 people homeless.

August 17 Sicily The capture of Messina marks Allied victory on Sicily; from there, the Allies attack the Italian peninsula.

Rescue of Mussolini

Adolf Hitler sent the SS officer Otto Skorzeny to rescue Mussolini from his imprisonment in a hotel high in the central Italian mountains. Using gliders, Skorzeny's assault force mounted a daring rescue and flew Mussolini to Vienna. He was appointed head of a puppet German state in northern Italy, which became the Republic of Salo.

The Italians sign the armistice with the Allies on September 3, 1943.

troops landed on July 9, 1943. The island's Italian defenders soon gave up, but German resistance was much stronger. Eventually, Allied numerical superiority won. The Germans retreated across the Strait of Messina to the mainland.

Italy Surrenders

Italy's politicians now sought a way out of the war. King Victor Emmanuel III sacked Mussolini on July 25, 1943. The former dictator was arrested and imprisoned in a remote hotel in the Apennine mountains. The Italians surrendered on September 3. Furious at the loss of his ally, Hitler sent troops to occupy northern Italy while the Germans retreating from Sicily seized the capital, Rome, and dug in at a defensive line to the south.

The Allies landed from Sicily at Salerno on September 9. They created a bridgehead and began to fight their way north.

Mussolini is escorted to a waiting aircraft after his rescue.

TIMELINE 1943 SEPTEMBER–DECEMBER

KEY: Pacific | Europe and North Africa | Sea and Air War

September

September 9 Italy U.S. and British troops land in southern Italy.

September 12 Italy German airborne troops led by Lieutenant Colonel Otto Skorzeny rescue Mussolini from imprisonment in a hotel high in the Italian mountains.

September 25 Soviet Union The Red Army recaptures Smolensk.

October

October 12–22 Italy The Allies advance slowly in bad weather toward German positions on the Gustav Line, in central Italy.

German resistance was strong, and it was not until May 1944 that the Allies broke through the defensive line at Monte Cassino. That breakthrough also liberated U.S. troops who had become trapped after landing behind German lines at Anzio. On June 5, 1944, U.S. troops entered Rome. Fighting in the north continued until April 1945, when the Germans surrendered.

The Fall of Italy

With the invasion of Sicily, Italian politicians feared that Italy might be next. To avoid destruction, they signed an armistice with the Allies on September 3. In response, German troops seized key targets across Italy. As the Germans completed their invasion, Allied troops arrived in the south. Fierce fighting followed. Although the Allies gained the upper hand, no immediate victory was forthcoming. Italy, however, was no longer a free agent: it was an occupied country.

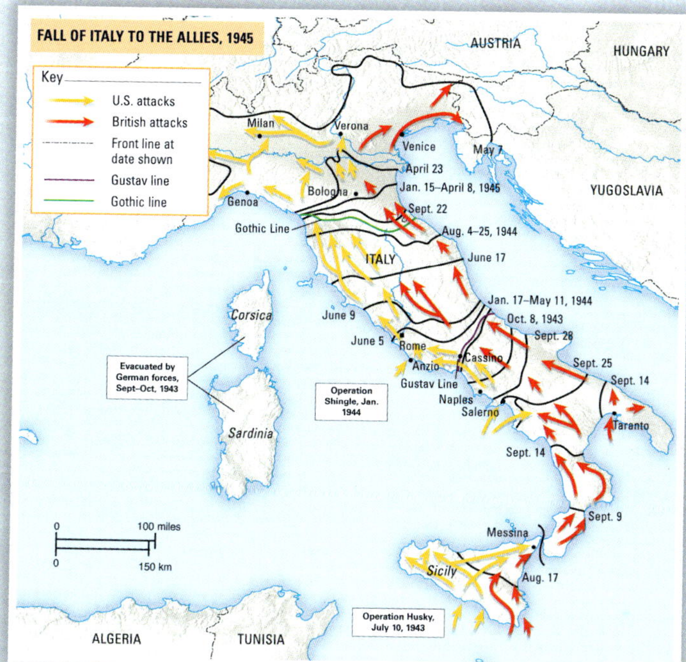

Main routes of the Allied advance through Italy.

November 6 Soviet Union
The Red Army captures Kiev, trapping the German Seventeenth Army in the Crimea.

November 20 Gilbert Islands
U.S. Marines land on Tawara and Bieto in the Gilbert Islands in the Pacific Ocean.

November 28 Iran
Winston Churchill, President Roosevelt, and Soviet leader Joseph Stalin meet in Tehran; they give priority to a cross-channel invasion of occupied Europe in May 1944.

December 26 Arctic Ocean
British warships sink German battleship *Scharnhorst* in the Battle of the North Cape.

November

December

Stalingrad

By late spring 1942, the Germans had recovered from near disaster outside Moscow during the freezing winter and had renewed their efforts to defeat Stalin.

During fighting, German infantry take cover in a Stalingrad trench.

TIMELINE 1944 JANUARY–APRIL

KEY: Pacific | Europe and North Africa | Sea and Air War

January

January 14–17 Leningrad German forces retreat. Some 830,000 civilians died in the three-year siege of the former capital.

January 22 Italy Allied troops land at Anzio, behind the Gustav Line, and meet little resistance; but U.S. General John Lucas orders his forces to dig in and create defensive positions.

January 30 Marshall Islands Americans begin an attack on the Marshall Islands in the Pacific.

February

February 4–24 Burma The Japanese launch operation Ha-Go to drive the Allies back to the border with India.

With Leningrad under siege in the north, in June 1942 the Germans launched Operation Blue into southern Russia. At first the German troops streamed across the vast Russian steppes. They met with little resistance. Stalin had been persuaded to surrender territory in order to gain time. Soviet forces withdrew as German forces advanced toward Stalingrad. The industrial city on the Volga River was strategically vital to halting the German advance.

← Soviet general Georgi Zhukov led the defense of Stalingrad.

KEY DATES

January 5, 1942 Stalin orders counterattack against German invaders.

June 28, 1942 Germans launch Operation Blue, summer offensive into southern Russia.

July 4-10, 1942 2-month siege ends with German capture of port of Sevastopol.

August 23, 1942 Raid by 600 German bombers on Stalingrad kills thousands.

November 19, 1942 Soviets launch attack to free Stalingrad. The rapid pincer movement traps Germans in the city and their front collapses.

December 19, 1942 Germans fail to rescue Sixth Army trapped in Stalingrad.

February 2, 1943 Siege ends when 93,000 German troops surrender.

← Soviet infantry fight in the ruins of Stalingrad.

March 20-22 Italy
Allied attacks fail to overcome Monte Cassino, part of the Gustav Line.

March

April

February 18-22
Marshall Islands
U.S. forces seize Eniwetok Atoll, completing the conquest of the islands.

Snipers at War

Stalingrad's ruins were ideal for snipers. Red Army sharpshooters picked off their victims from hidden positions. They lay immobile for hours and used their telescopic sights to find a target. Male and female Russian snipers killed hundreds of German officers and spread great fear. They were rewarded with improved food and quarters.

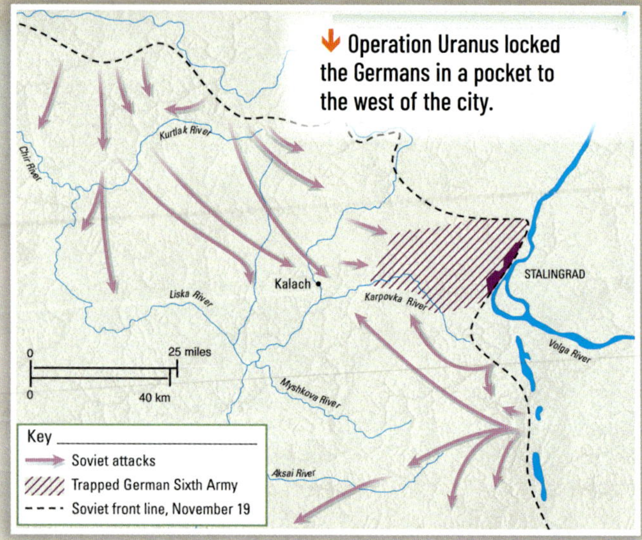

Operation Uranus locked the Germans in a pocket to the west of the city.

Under Attack

In August 1942, the Luftwaffe began bombing Stalingrad, reducing much of the city to rubble. As German troops entered the city they met stubborn resistance. Fighting raged through the ruins. Soviet civilians lived in cellars and sewers, surviving on food they found in the pockets of the dead. The Germans could not, however, dislodge Soviet troops from the small areas of the city they still held, despite almost continual bombardment.

The Soviet sniper Vasily Zaitsev (on the far left) killed more than 200 Germans.

TIMELINE 1944 MAY–AUGUST

KEY: Pacific | Europe and North Africa | Sea and Air War

May

May 9 Soviet Union The Red Army liberates the Black Sea port of Sevastopol.

May 11-18 Italy The Allies break through the Gustav Line near Monte Cassino.

June

June 3 Italy German troops abandon Rome; it is occupied by U.S. troops on June 5.

June 6 Northern France D-Day. The Allied invasion of Normandy, Operation Overlord, begins with paratroopers landing to seize key targets and amphibious landings on five beaches. By the end of the day, the Allies have a beachhead in Europe at the cost of 2,500 dead.

June 19-21 Philippine Sea The "Great Marianas Turkey Shoot." The Japanese lose three aircraft carriers and 460 aircraft in the Battle of the Philippine Sea.

Soviet infantry advance through the ruins of Stalingrad.

German attacks grew less frequent and were all but over by November 12.

Defeat of the Sixth Army

The Soviets began a counterattack. On November 19, General Georgi Zhukov launched a rapid pincer movement, Operation Uranus, that trapped the Germans in the city. They suffered from bitterly cold weather and a shortage of food. Meanwhile, Hitler called off plans to rescue the Sixth Army. The troops were on their own.

Surrender in the Snow

German commander Friedrich Paulus asked Hitler to be allowed to open negotiations with the Soviets. Hitler refused and made it clear that he wanted Paulus to commit suicide. Instead, Paulus surrendered his 93,000 men on February 2, 1943. The Soviet Union had won a great victory.

Disobeying Hitler

On January 30, 1943, Hitler promoted the commander of the Sixth Army, Friedrich Paulus, to field marshal. Rather than a reward, however, the promotion was a signal that Paulus should commit suicide rather than surrender. No German officer of such a rank had ever surrendered. Paulus ignored Hitler; he surrendered and spent the rest of the war as a prisoner.

Friedrich Paulus was released by the Soviets in 1953. While in captivity, he had become a critic of the Nazi leadership.

June 22 Soviet Union
With superior numbers, the Red Army launches Operation Bagration against German Army Group Center.

June 30 Britain
To date, 2,000 V1 "flying bombs" have been launched against British targets, mostly London.

July

July 20 Germany
German officers try to kill Hitler. Count Schenk von Stauffenberg plants a bomb but it fails to kill Hitler. The failure leads to the execution of dozens of suspects.

August

August 1 Poland
The Warsaw Uprising: 38,000 soldiers of the Polish Home Army fight the Germans.

August 25 France
General Dietrich von Choltitz, commander of the German garrison in Paris, surrenders the city to the Allies.

The Holocaust

The German state's attack on the Jewish people was the worst war crime in history.

Hitler had risen to prominence in Germany in the 1920s with a promise to overturn the Versailles settlement of 1919. He also maintained a hatred of Jewish people that he expressed in his book *Mein Kampf* (My Struggle), written in 1924. Hitler characterized Jews as being part of an international conspiracy that included communism and American capitalism. These ideas were contradictory but they still had great appeal.

1

Mass Slaughter

Hitler came to power in 1933 and his government passed laws against Jewish people. In 1938 Nazis attacked the homes and businesses of Jews during *Kristallnacht* (Night of Broken Glass). After the outbreak of World War II, even harsher measures were taken against Jews, especially in occupied Poland, which had one of the largest Jewish populations in Europe. When German forces invaded the Soviet Union in 1941, *Einsatzgruppen* (Special Units) followed the troops and massacred hundreds of thousands of Jews. In 1942, Germany began the "Final Solution," a policy to wipe out Jews in areas under German control. Other groups, such as Romany people, were included in this attempt at genocide. Over six million people died in what is now called the Holocaust.

3

KEY DATES

1924 Hitler writes *Mein Kampf*, which describes the Jewish people as "germs."

September 1935 The Nuremberg laws are passed. They severely restrict the liberties of Jews in Germany.

November 9, 1938 Kristallnacht. Jewish homes and businesses in Germany are physically attacked by Nazi thugs.

September 29, 1941 The massacre at Babi Yar. German forces invading the Soviet Union kill over 30,000 Jewish people near Kiev.

January 1942 The Wansee Conference. At a lakeside near Berlin, the decision to kill all Jews in Europe, the "Final Solution," is taken by the Nazi leaders.

January 27, 1945 Auschwitz concentration camp is liberated by Soviet forces. It is estimated that 1.1 million people died there from the first gassing of victims in 1941.

1 The main gate at Auschwitz concentration camp. The German words across the top mean "work sets you free."

2 The front cover of Hitler's *Mein Kampf*. The book laid out a deeply anti-semitic world view that Hitler fully believed in.

3 Auschwitz concentration camp, the center of a network of work and death camps. Trains delivered victims to the camp until late 1944.

4 The Nuremberg trials. Nazi leaders were formally tried for the crimes that the Nazi state had committed during World War II.

5 A synagogue in the aftermath of Kristallnacht in 1938. This was the most stark warning of Hitler's deadly intentions toward the Jewish people.

D-Day: Operation Overlord

The D-Day landings remain the greatest amphibious assault of all time. The landings hastened Nazi Germany's defeat, but were a major gamble by the western Allies.

← U.S. infantry land on Omaha Beach late on June 6, 1944.

TIMELINE **1944 SEPTEMBER–DECEMBER**

KEY: Pacific | Europe and North Africa | Sea and Air War

September

September 2 Finland
Finland accepts a peace treaty with the Soviet Union and severs relations with Germany.

September 17 Holland
Operation Market Garden. The Allies suffer heavy losses as paratroopers try to seize key bridges.

September 22–25 Holland British paratroopers retreat from Arnhem.

October

October 2 Poland
After a two-month battle, the last Poles in Warsaw surrender to the Germans; 150,000 Poles have died.

In early June 1944, southern Britain became a vast army camp as the Allied forces prepared for the most complex military operation ever attempted: landing huge numbers of troops across the Channel.

← Loaded landing craft speed toward the Normandy coast.

The Allies had selected Normandy in northern France as the site for the landings. They sent fake signals by radio in order to divert the Germans into believing that the invasion would come farther to the northeast.

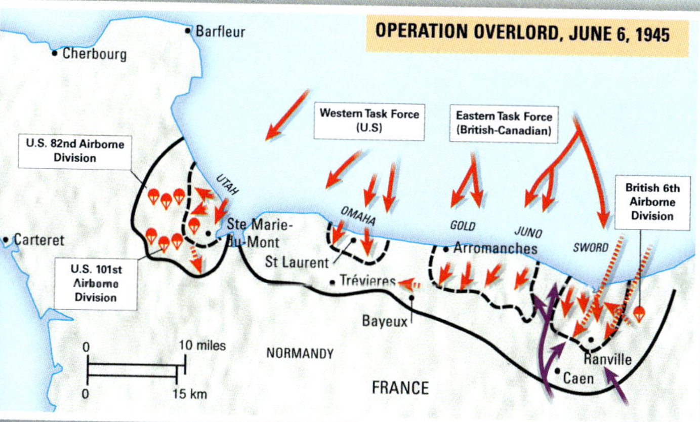

← The five invasion beaches were secured on D-Day, but the Allies did not move inland.

KEY DATES

January 1943 Planning for D-Day begins.

May 29, 1944 Allied troops begin moving to ports along the south coast of England.

June 3, 1944 All ready, waiting for weather to turn favorable.

June 5, 1944 7,000 warships leave for Normandy.

June 6, 1944 D-Day. Allied invasion of Normandy, Operation Overlord, begins.

June 10, 1944 German soldiers kill 642 civilians in Oradour-sur-Glane as retaliation for attacks on a panzer division by the French Resistance.

June 13, 1944 27 British tanks are destroyed in battle in Villers-Bocage, Normandy.

August 25, 1944 German garrison commander in Paris surrenders to Allies.

October 20 Philippines
The U.S. Sixth Army lands on Leyte Island in the Philippines; U.S. General Douglas MacArthur is able to fulfill the promise he had made two years earlier: "I shall return."

October 23–26 Philippines
The Japanese Combined Fleet is defeated heavily at the wide-ranging Battle of Leyte Gulf.

November

December

December 16 Belgium
Hitler begins Operation Watch on the Rhine, which aims to capture Antwerp. The Germans advance in thick fog. They are stopped by U.S. paratroopers in Bastogne.

Dwight D. Eisenhower

People doubted the Allied Supreme Commander had enough experience to lead the invasion. Eisenhower proved them wrong, partly thanks to his combat experience in North Africa. His strategy of advancing on a broad front in northwest Europe in late 1944 is widely judged to have been correct.

U.S. troops help a fellow soldier on Omaha Beach.

On June 3, bad weather delayed Operation Overlord. On June 5, an improvement in the weather for about 24 hours allowed some 7,000 warships and landing craft to set out for Normandy.

D-Day

Shortly after midnight on June 6, U.S. and British paratroopers successfully landed inland from the five landing beaches to capture vital roads and bridges. The actual landings took place after an artillery bombardment from Allied warships and an attack from Allied bombers on German positions.

The Allied High Command for D-Day included Eisenhower (front, center) and Field Marshal Bernard Montgomery (front, right).

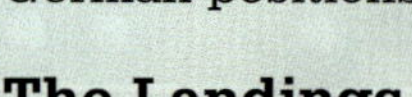

The Landings

The landings met different degrees of resistance. U.S. troops landed on Utah Beach at

TIMELINE 1945 JANUARY–MARCH

KEY: Pacific | Europe and North Africa | Sea and Air War

January

January 27 Poland
The Red Army advancing west liberates the death camp at Auschwitz.

January 28 Belgium
The German Ardennes offensive costs about 100,000 German lives, and about 81,000 U.S. casualties.

January 30 Germany
Soviet forces reach the Oder River, only 100 miles (160 km) from Berlin.

February

February 3 Philippines
U.S. forces enter Manila, capital of the Philippines; Japanese forces virtually destroy the city before they are pushed out.

February 4 Soviet Union
Stalin, Roosevelt, and Churchill meet at Yalta to decide the division of postwar Europe.

6:31 a.m., just a minute behind schedule. By nightfall on D-Day, some 23,000 men and 1,700 vehicles had gone ashore with few casualties. Only 10 miles (16 km) to the east, however, Omaha Beach was nearly a disaster. Due to Allied mistakes, some 2,300 U.S. troops were killed.

Anglo-Canadian Landings

On Gold, Sword, and Juno beaches, which stretched for 25 miles (40 km), British and Canadian forces met relatively little resistance. By late morning, all three invasion groups were also pushing inland. They were helped because the Germans had held their panzer divisions farther to the northeast.

However, despite the massive success of D-Day the Allies had failed in one goal. They had not pushed inland as far as they had hoped. This had repercussions in the following weeks as the Germans fought back with tenacity. The Allies still faced weeks of bloody combat in order to break out of Normandy and advance first north into Belgium and then across the Rhine River into Germany itself.

The Resistance

The Allied invasion was supported by the French Resistance. British and U.S. agents went to Normandy before D-Day to deliver weapons and get intelligence. They helped organize sabotage attacks on railroads that the Germans might use to get reinforcements to the coast. Railroad workers also staged go-slows. The Germans believed it was this action, not the Resistance or Allied bombings, that made France's rail system unworkable.

Members of the maquis and Free French troops during the invasion of Normandy.

February 13–14 Germany
British bombers bomb Dresden, creating a massive firestorm that kills at least 50,000 people.

February 14 Germany
As the Red Army advances, half of the 2.3 million population of German East Prussia flees west. Thousands die from cold or exhaustion.

February 17 Iwo Jima
U.S. Marines land on the island of Iwo Jima, which they capture after a month of heavy fighting.

March

March 7 Japan
A U.S. bombing raid on Tokyo kills 100,000 people and destroys a large area of the Japanese capital.

March 23 Germany
British and U.S. forces start to cross the Rhine River. German troops offer little resistance.

Bombing Nazi Germany

The Allies wanted to attack German industry from the air, but at first were unsure about the best tactics.

Early in World War II, German aircraft inflicted massive damage on enemy cities, notably Warsaw in 1939 and Rotterdam in 1940. During the autumn and winter of 1940, German bombers then attacked British cities.

By Day or By Night?

In 1940 and 1941, Britain's Royal Air Force (RAF) made raids on German cities, but with little success. The United States entered the war in December 1941, and American and British strategists discussed how they could weaken German industrial output. American officers decided to concentrate on daylight bombing raids, so the targets could be seen. This policy initially led to heavy losses, particularly in the Schweinfurt Raid of October 1943, when 22 percent of the aircrew were lost.

Although U.S. bombers were equipped with many machine guns, the breakthrough came when long-distance fighters carrying special tanks for fuel accompanied the bombers. This enabled the U.S. Air Force (USAAF) to make effective raids all over Germany.

Meanwhile, the RAF decided to make night attacks. Led by Arthur Harris, the RAF attacked cities in massive bombing raids intended to weaken civilians, creating firestorms that destroyed vast areas of housing. In one set of raids in February 1945, USAAF and RAF planes attacked the city of Dresden, flattening the city and killing up to 25,000 people.

KEY DATES

April 26, 1937 German and Italian planes destroy the town of Guernica in northern Spain during the Spanish Civil War. This acts as an example of the damage that bombing raids could inflict.

September 7, 1940 German bombers attack London, the beginning of what the British called the Blitz.

September 1941 A British report on bombing explains how it is designed to destroy cities and to break civilian morale.

May 30, 1942 First "Thousand Bomber Raid" on the German city of Cologne.

February 1944 U.S. bombers and their escorting fighters make a series of raids known as "Big Week," from which the German air defenses will never recover.

1945 The United States Strategic Bombing survey estimates that Allied bombers dropped a total of 1,415,745 tons of bombs in Germany during the war.

1 The ruins of the city of Dresden after the devastating raids of February 1945. The morality of these raids is still debated.

2 Curtis LeMay, head of the 3rd Air Division, congratulates a bomber crew. LeMay later ordered the devastating fire raids on Japan.

3 B-17 Flying Fortresses on their way to Germany. The B-17 dropped more bombs than any other U.S. aircraft during World War II.

4 British Lancaster bombers head toward Germany. Over 7,000 Lancasters were produced during World War II.

The Fall of Germany

At the start of 1945, the Third Reich was being crushed between forces from both east and west. Armageddon was about to descend upon the people of Germany.

A Soviet soldier raises the Red Flag of the Soviet Union above the Reichstag in Berlin.

TIMELINE **1945 APRIL–JUNE**

KEY: Pacific | Europe and North Africa | Politics

April

April 12 United States
President Roosevelt dies of a brain hemorrhage; Vice President Harry S. Truman takes over as president.

April 16 Germany
The Soviets attack Berlin; they vastly outnumber the Germans in terms of troops, tanks, weapons, and aircraft.

April 28 Italy
Mussolini is shot dead by partisans as he tries to flee to Austria.

April 29 Italy
German forces in Italy finally surrender to the Allies.

April 30 Germany
Hitler and Eva Braun commit suicide in their bunker in Berlin.

May

May 2 Germany
The Reichstag falls to the Red Army after a savage three-day battle.

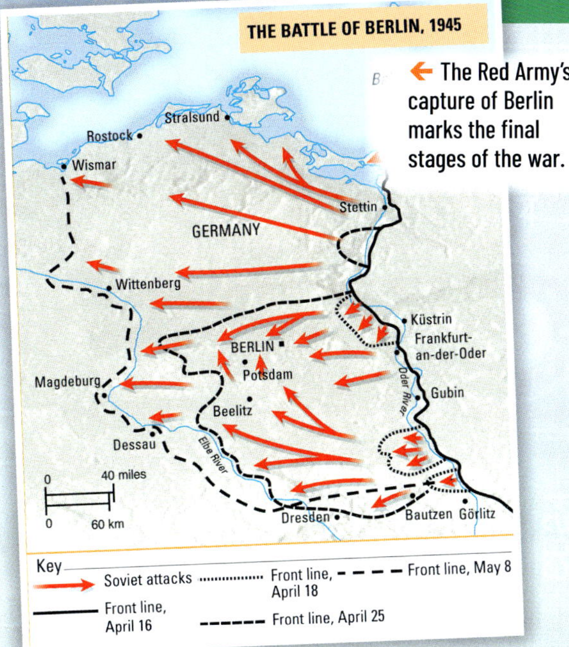

The Red Army's capture of Berlin marks the final stages of the war.

In February 1945, the Allies began the conquest of Germany. The British and Americans advanced from the west, while in the east, the Red Army was already positioned on the German border.

On February 8, 1945, an artillery bombardment began an attack on the Rhine River. After heavy fighting, the Allies succeeded in crossing the Rhine and establishing bridgeheads in three places.

KEY DATES

January 12-17, 1945
Red Army begins its advance against Germany.

February 4, 1945 Churchill, Roosevelt, and Stalin meet at Yalta to discuss postwar Europe. Germany is to be divided into four administrative zones.

February 13-14, 1945 Allies bomb Dresden, killing at least 50,000 civilians.

April 16, 1945 Red Army reaches Berlin.

April 25, 1945 Red Army surrounds Berlin.

April 30, 1945 Hitler and Eva Braun commit suicide.

May 2, 1945 Berlin falls to the Soviets after three days of fierce fighting.

May 8, 1945 Victory in Europe (VE) Day; the Allies accept the surrender of Germany.

July 17-August 2, 1945
New U.S. President Harry S. Truman and new British Prime Minister Clement Attlee meet Stalin at Potsdam to discuss postwar policy in Europe.

May 3 Burma
Sweeping Allied advances take Rangoon and liberate Burma.

May 8 Europe
Victory in Europe (VE) Day; the Allies accept the unconditional surrender of Germany.

June

June 22 Okinawa
Japanese resistance ends on the island of Okinawa; the battle has cost the Japanese 110,000 dead.

Inside Hitler's Bunker

From April 20 to April 30, 1945, Hitler lived in the Führerbunker with Eva Braun and many staff. By this time, he was a broken man. Even his closest allies began to desert him. On April 29, Hitler learned that Russian forces were close by. He married Eva Braun. The next day, the pair committed suicide. Braun took cyanide, while Hitler shot himself.

➔ Russian troops look on as the Reichstag smolders after the fall of Berlin in 1945.

Political Decisions

At the Yalta Conference in February 1945, the Allied politicians had agreed that the Soviet Red Army would capture Berlin. Eisenhower decided to halt at the Elbe River, about 45 miles (70 km) west of the city. There, on April 25, 1945, a U.S. patrol met up with Soviet forces. The Allies' eastern and western advances had come together.

The Red Army Advances

The Red Army had assembled nearly four million men for its advance into Germany. Resisting the largest single offensive of the war were four battle-weary German formations of about 600,000 men. German resistance in East Prussia soon collapsed, followed by the Hungarian capital Budapest. By April 13, the Red Army had taken the Austrian capital, Vienna.

➔ One of the last images of Hitler shows him with Hitler Youth boys in April 1945.

TIMELINE 1945 JULY–SEPTEMBER

KEY: Pacific | Europe and North Africa | Politics

July

July 17–August 2 Germany
U.S. President Harry S. Truman, Stalin, and new British Prime Minister Clement Attlee meet at Potsdam to discuss postwar policy in Europe.

August

August 6 Japan
A B-29 drops an atomic bomb on the Japanese city of Hiroshima, killing 70,000 and injuring a similar number.

August 9 Manchuria
A huge Soviet offensive begins against the Japanese Kwantung Army in Asia.

The Battle of Berlin

Inside Berlin, Hitler had scraped together almost every male to defend the city. The one million defenders included many poorly trained members of the Volkssturm, a home guard of older men and young teenagers. Hitler himself had retreated to his bunker beneath the Chancellery, the political center of Berlin. By April 25, Berlin was surrounded. German resistance remained strong; the SS threatened to hang any man who was not fighting the Allies.

End of the Reich

By April 27, the Germans held only 15 square miles (38 sq km) of the city. Hitler ordered resistance to continue. By April 30, the Soviets had fought their way to within half a mile (800 m) of the Chancellery. Hitler married his mistress, Eva Braun, and then committed suicide.

On May 2, Berlin's commandant, Lieutenant-General Karl Weidling, surrendered. Five days later, Germany itself signed a total surrender. World War II in Europe was over.

New Yorkers celebrate Victory in Europe (VE) Day on May 8, 1945.

The Surrender

Hitler's death and the surrender of Berlin did not stop the fighting in Europe. Admiral Dönitz, who now led Germany, wanted as many Germans as possible to escape, so delayed surrender as long as he could. At 2:41 a.m. on May 7, the Germans signed the surrender, which came into effect at one minute past midnight on May 9.

Fighting continued until May 11 in Austria and Czechoslovakia, but the Allies could celebrate victory in Europe.

August 9 Japan
An atomic bomb is dropped on Nagasaki, killing 35,000 people. The Japanese decide that they must surrender.

August 15 Japan
Victory over Japan (VJ) Day; the Japanese surrender is announced to grateful crowds in the USA.

August 23 Manchuria
The Soviet campaign against the Japanese ends in total victory.

September

September 2 Japan
Aboard the U.S. battleship *Missouri* in Tokyo Bay, Japanese officials sign the Instrument of Surrender; World War II is finally over.

World War II to Cold War

Victory in World War II was followed by a tense standoff between western democracies and the Soviet Union.

The soldiers and civilians in the Allied nations felt a great wave of relief in May 1945 as the war in Europe ended. U.S. and Russian troops met on the River Elbe and shook hands. However, the question of how Europe should be organized after the war led to disputes. The United States and Britain wanted to establish democracy in the areas that they occupied, whereas Soviet leader Joseph Stalin was determined to create communist regimes in the areas his armies had marched into.

1

Berlin Airlift

The USA offered assistance to western Europe in the form of Marshall Aid, while Stalin made sure that almost all the countries occupied by the Red Army were unable to leave Soviet control.

Germany was divided between the area occupied by the Red Army in the east and the larger western portion. The capital, Berlin, was in the Red Army zone, but divided between the victorious powers. Stalin tried to force western troops out of Berlin in 1948 by cutting land routes. The west supplied the city by air in the "Berlin Airlift" and in 1949 Stalin backed off. By now, however, there was an open rift between the former allies. A Cold War had begun that would last until the 1990s.

2

KEY DATES

June 1948 The Berlin Airlift begins.

October 1949 Communist Party under Mao Zhedong takes over China.

April 1949 NATO (North Atlantic Treaty Organization) is founded.

1950 War breaks out in Korea as the communist north invades the south. U.S. forces defend South Korea while China sends in its Red Army troops to help North Korea.

1955 The Warsaw Pact is created as a communist response to NATO in Europe.

1956 Red Army tanks enter Hungary and put down rebels calling for democracy.

1962 The Cuban Missile Crisis. There is almost nuclear war as the Soviet Union tries to establish rocket bases on Cuba.

1 Aircraft line up at Templehof airfield in Berlin during the airlift that kept the city supplied when Stalin cut land routes.

2 Anxious West Berliners watch as supply aircraft head into the city soon after the airlift was announced.

3 Days of celebration. U.S. troops and Red Army soldiers congratulate each other on victory over Germany in 1945.

4 A turning point for the world came in 1949, when Chairman Mao announced the formation of the communist People's Republic of China.

5 Three Kennedy brothers (from left to right: Bobby, Edward, and John). John F. Kennedy was president during the most dangerous phase of the Cold War, the Cuban Missile Crisis of 1962.

Glossary

appeasement Avoiding conflict by giving in to someone's demands.

civil war A war between two opposing groups of citizens of the same country.

commandos Special forces soldiers.

convoy A number of ships or vehicles traveling together.

corps A military unit made up of several divisions.

counterattack An attack by a defending force.

destroyer A small, fast warship.

division An army unit made up of 15,000 to 20,000 soldiers.

evacuation The removal of people from a dangerous area.

expeditionary force An army sent to serve abroad.

garrison A military post

ghetto Part of a city where Jews were forced to live.

liberate To set free.

marine A soldier based on a ship who fights on land.

morale The emotional well-being of people.

occupation Military control of part of a country by forces from another.

panzer German word for a tank.

paratrooper A soldier who jumps from an aircraft with a parachute.

partisan A person fighting behind enemy lines who is not a regular soldier.

pocket battleship A powerful warship smaller than a battleship.

Reichstag The German parliament.

retaliation Revenge for a previous event.

strategic Something that is useful in achieving a long-term goal.

strategy A long-term plan of action.

surrender To stop fighting and give in to the enemy.

U-boat A German submarine.

uprising A revolt against a ruler.

"wolf pack" A group of 15 to 20 German U-boats.

Further Resources

Books

Doeden, Matt. *World War II Resistance Fighters.* Lerner Publishing Group, 2018.

Doeden, Matt. *World War II Code Talkers.* Lerner Publishing Group, 2019.

Ellis, Catherine. *Key Figures of World War II.* Rosen Publishing, 2016.

Hardyman, Robyn. *What Caused World War II?.* Gareth Stevens, 2017.

Harriot, Emma. *Did Anything Good Come Out of World War II?,* Rosen Publishing, 2016.

Hunter, Nick. *World War II (Frontline Soldiers and Their Families).* Gareth Stevens, 2016.

National Geographic. *Everything World War II.* National Geographic Kids, 2021.

Smithsonian Museum. *World War II Map by Map.* Dorling Kindersley, 2019.

Smithsonian Museum. *World War II The Definitive Visual History.* Dorling Kindersley, 2015.

Zabecki, David. *The German War Machine in World War II.* ABC CLIO, 2019.

Websites

americanhistory.si.edu/exhibitions/price-of-freedom
A site that covers all U.S. military history from the 18th century.

www.bbc.co.uk/history/worldwars/wwtwo/
A general World War II resource.

www.ibiblio.org/pha/
A collection of primary World War II source materials.

war-experience.org/wwii-timeline/
Timelines and other information about World War II from the Second World War Experience Center.

www.secondworldwar.co.uk
A general World War II resource, including important dates, casualty figures, events, biographies and trivia.

Index